Love of Allah:
Experience the Beauty of Salah

'The sweetness of this life lies in *remembering* Him,
the sweetness of the next life lies in *seeing* Him!'

Mishari al-Kharraz

Edited by
A.B. al-Mehri

THE QUR'ĀN PROJECT
www.quranproject.org

Duas Seeking the Love of Allah

اللَّهُمَّ إِنِّ أَسْأَلُكَ حُبَّكَ، وَحُبَّ مَنْ يُحِبُّكَ، وَالعَمَلَ الَّذي يُبَلِّغُني حُبَّكَ، اللَّهُمَّ اجْعَلْ حُبَّكَ أَحَبَّ إِلَيَّ مِنْ نَفْسي وَأَهْلي، وَمِنَ المَاءِ البَارد

"O Allah, I ask You for Your love and the love of those who love You and love of the action which will make me reach Your love. O Allah make Your love more beloved to me than myself, my family and cold water"[1]

اللَّهُمَّ ارْزُقْني حُبَّكَ وَحُبَّ مَنْ يَنْفَعُني حُبُّهُ عِنْدَكَ، اللَّهُمَّ مَا رَزَقْتَني مِمَّا أُحِبُّ فَاجْعَلْهُ قُوَّةً لي فيمَا تُحِبُّ، اللَّهُمَّ وَمَا زَوَيْتَ عَنِّي مِمَّا أُحِبُّ فَاجْعَلْهُ فَرَاغًا لي فيمَا تُحِبُّ

"O Allah, provide me with Your love and the love of those whose love will benefit me with You. O Allah, that which you have provided me of that which I love, then make it strength for me in that which you love. O Allah, that which you have removed of what I love, then make it a free space for me for that which you love."[2]

اللهُمَّ اجْعَلْ حُبَّكَ أَحَبَّ الْأَشْيَاءِ إِلَيَّ وَاجْعَلْ خَوْفَكَ أَخْوَفَ الْأَشْيَاءِ إِلَيَّ وَاقْطَعْ عَنِّي حَاجَاتِ الدُّنْيَا بِالشَّوْقِ إِلَى لِقَائِكَ وَإِذَا أَقْرَرْتَ أَعْيُنَ أَهْلِ الدُّنْيَا مِنْ دُنْيَاهُمْ فَأَقِرَّ عَيْني مِنْ عِبَادَتك

"O Allah, make your love the most beloved of things to me, and your fear the most fearful of things to me and sever for me the needs of the dunya by longing for meeting You and when You give delight to the eyes of the people of the world in their dunya, then give my eye delight in your worship"[3]

---

[1] Tirmidhi #3490 [Hasan Ghareeb].
[2] Tirmidhi #3491.
[3] Abu Naym, *Hilyat alAwliya* – [All three Duas quoted in 'Jami al-Uloom wal-Hikam' by Ibn Rajab al-Hanbali].

Editors Preface

This book is a compilation of the Ramadan 2008 e-mail series, "Taste It!", which summarized the popular lectures "How to Taste the True Beauty of Salah" presented by Mishari al-Kharraz. The following publication has been edited in order for it to be published into book form along with the inclusion of Arabic text.

As the author notes about our Creator, 'The sweetness of this life lies in *remembering* Him, the sweetness of the next life lies in *seeing* Him! The next time you proceed for prayer, go because you *love Him*, go because you *miss Him* and long to be with Him. Feel your heart flutter. Only then, will you be on your way to attaining that inner peace and comfort Salah was prescribed for.'

As with all Qur'an Project publications – there is no copyright and no rights reserved. Any part of this publication may be reproduced in any language, stored in a retrieval system or transmitted in any form or by any means, electrical, mechanical, photocopying, recording or otherwise without our permission, as long as no changes are made to the material. Please kindly send us notification for our records.

You are also able to download a free PDF version of this book at www.quranproject.org.

May Allah [swt] grant us the most blessed conditions in our Salah and achieve the status of being amongst the most beloved to The Beloved Himself. O Allah, bless us with Your Love, the love of whom You Love and the love of deeds which bring us closer to Your Love. Please save us from the Fire, Forgive us for every sin and bless us and our families to be with You in the highest places of Jannah [ameen].

A.B. al-Mehri
The Qur'an Project
Birmingham, U.K.

ISBN 9798433844995

Do you sometimes feel that your Salah [prayer] is not quite having the effect it is supposed to on you and your life? Have you ever considered that perhaps it is because we are not giving it its due importance? It seems we have lost [or were never taught] that ability to 'connect' in Salah that makes all the difference in its effect on us.

Consider the following examples of those who came before us:

- The Muslims once headed out with the Prophet ﷺ on way to battle. During the trip the Prophet ordered two companions, one of the Ansar [helpers] and one of the Muhajireen [emigrants], to stand guard over them. As they did the Muhajir decided to rest while the Ansari chose to stand in prayer. Along came a disbeliever and cast an arrow striking the Ansari in the chest. The Ansari pulled out the arrow and continued in prayer. The disbeliever struck him with a second arrow. Again the Ansari removed it and continued his prayer. A third arrow was cast but now the Ansari could no longer stand and finally fell bleeding into his Ruku [bowing position] and Sujood [prostration]. The aggressor fled as the Muhajir rushed to his brother's aid, "Subhanallah! Why didn't you alert me from the first arrow?" The Ansari replied, "I was in the middle of a [beautiful] Surah and didn't wish to interrupt my recitation of it."

- Imam Bukhari was once stung by a wasp 17 times while standing in prayer. When he finished, he felt some discomfort and asked if anyone was aware of what caused it.

- Ibn Zubair stood firm and unflinching in his prayer while catapults fired upon the ground he stood on.

- It was said that when Ali washed in preparation for prayer, he always went pale and trembled with anxiety as he thought of himself about to stand before his Lord.

- Another companion needed an amputation. He requested that it be performed while he was engaged in Salah.

- An entire wall collapsed in the mosque that one companion was praying in, but he was too engrossed to realize what happened till his prayer was completed.

How did they attain that level of pleasure and inner peace that Salah is meant to inspire? Is it possible for us to reach that level too? How can we make our Salah effective? This is what we hope to learn.

Outlook is Key

Now before any change in us can take place, we need to re-examine our outlook on prayer.

Ask yourself: Why do I pray? Is it just because I have to? Is it just to get this daily duty out of the way and over with? Or maybe it is because everyone just does it so I do it too?

It's time to make a change. We need to start praying out of sincere **Love**. Pray out of *longing* to be with the one you love. Pray for the peace and comfort that comes from being with the one you love.

There are 3 reasons which make you love someone:
1. Either because that someone is beautiful!
2. Or because that someone always deals kindly with you.
3. Or because that someone has done many favours for you.

Think of Allah now. He is all of the above and more, isn't He? Doesn't He then deserve to be the most worthy of our love over everything and anyone else? To truly love Allah [swt] is to truly taste the greatest love in existence! It is to truly taste the beauty of faith:

As to Allah's beauty, look around at all that is beautiful in creation, be it inner or outer beauty. It is all but a small hint to the ultimate beauty He beholds. If every person was created with the beauty of Prophet Yusuf and this total beauty was combined with the beauty of everything we see around us - all this in comparison to the beauty of Allah, would be like that of a weak candle light to the brightness of the sun! And Allah's beauty is unique, for it's coupled with everlasting glory! And just think. He sets this Most Beautiful, Glorious Face to yours when you stand in prayer!

Allah's beauty is so immense that we cannot see Him in this world, for if He were to manifest to us His glory, it would burn everything in existence! Recall what happened to Prophet Musa when he once asked to see Allah [swt]. Allah [swt] said, *"You cannot see Me. But look upon the mountain, if it remains firm in place then you will be able to see Me."*

To this, Allah manifested Himself to the mountain, and the mountain crumbled in total annihilation! Musa collapsed, and fainted [see 7:143]. This was what happened to Musa when he only saw *the mountain* which saw Allah's beauty. So imagine if it was a direct sight!

As to Allah's kindness and favours upon us, just close your eyes momentarily to appreciate just the gift of sight alone. If we were to count His favours upon us, never will we be able to enumerate them. And sometimes we gripe when a favour has not been granted us. Don't we then realize in hindsight, that it was much better for us this way? The denial of this favour, we realize later, was a favour in itself. For Allah has nothing but good.

And imagine. When we dare and sin against Him, we sin using the very gifts and blessings He has given us! But out of His love and mercy for us, He continues to guard over us and protect us, even while we're in the act! You will not find anyone more kind; you will not find anyone more giving. You will not find anyone more worthy of your love than He.

Remember this: The sweetness of this life lies in *remembering* Him, the sweetness of the next life lies in *seeing* Him! The next time you proceed for prayer, go because you *love Him*, go because you *miss Him* and long to be with Him. Feel your heart flutter. Only then, will you be on your way to attaining that inner peace and comfort Salah was prescribed for.

Upon "Allahu Akbar"

اللهُ أَكْبَرُ

So what really happens at "*Allahu Akbar*"?

But before we go into what really happens. Have you ever wondered why we start our prayer with "Allahu Akbar"? Why don't we say "Subhanallah", for instance? "Allahu Akbar" is the key phrase because with it we affirm that Allah, before Whom we are about to stand, is greater than anything occupying us at that moment. He is greater than our job, greater than our business, greater than our sleep, our bills, our family and our children, greater than all that troubles or preoccupies us. And why do we raise our hands with it? We raise our hands to *throw all of that behind us*. We raise our hands, as a gesture of *complete surrender*.

When one stands to pray Allah commands, "Raise the veils from between Me and my servant!" From the instant you proclaim "Allahu Akbar", Allah now sets His Beautiful Glorious Face to yours ready and engaged, with you. And He doesn't turn away from you,...*unless you do* - That's when either you turn away with your head/sight, or drift in heart and mind back to worldly matters. And if you turn or drift, He calls to you: "[you turn] To what is better than I?" and orders for the veils, to draw back down.

When you announce "Allahu Akbar", imagine that you are before the cameras and the red "ON THE AIR" button has now been switched on. But it is not ordinary people who are watching you, it is The King Himself. In His hands is everything you are and everything you will ever be. In His hands is the entire universe, running in perfect order. Nothing, however big or small, escapes His control. How will you stand? Feel your heart race!

Upon "Allahu Akbar" and as we proceed to recite; any bad deeds committed by our faculties suddenly begin to float up...up until they reach our head and shoulders. Subsequently, with every Ruku [bow] and Sujood [prostration] we move to, these sins fall off and away, scattered and gone! [All the more reason for us to hold in those humbling positions longer before our Lord.]

With "Allahu Akbar", things we were permitted to do just moments before suddenly become forbidden...like food, drink, talk, unnecessary movement. What happened? What is different now? Well, these acts are not befitting of a

7

meeting of this nature. For the servant has answered the call and now stands in humility before his Master. You are on a much higher level now. Focus. Are you still drifting? This is why we repeat these great words, "Allahu Akbar" as we move to each position. It is a reminder, and a new chance to refocus.

Salute the King & Expel the Intruder

Now you have officially entered Salah when you proclaimed "Allahu Akbar". You lower your gaze to the place of your Sujood [prostration] and you now place your hands right over left and close to your heart/lower chest. Why? Imagine that you have walked into a royal palace and you enter upon a group of people standing in the distance. Some in the group fix their gaze boldly at you with their arms comfortably at their sides. The other group stands with their gaze to the ground and their hands clasped in front of them.

Just from the way they stand; you will easily be able to distinguish the royalty from the palace servants, wouldn't you? It is not befitting of us, as servants, but to stand in a position of humility when we face Our Lord. It is humbling when we remember who we really are before Him.

But let us remember that the humility due to Allah is a *dignifying* humility because, in essence, it liberates us from the undue humility to fellow man. As the Prophet ﷺ said, *"The one who humbles himself before Allah is elevated [by Allah] in honor!"*

It is only proper now, to *salute* The King:

سُبْحَانَكَ اللَّهُمَّ وَبِحَمْدِكَ وَتَبَارَكَ اسْمُكَ وَتَعَالَى جَدُّكَ وَلاَ إِلَه غَيْرُكَ

"How perfect You are O Allah, praise be to You. Blessed is Your name and lofty is Your position and non has the right to be worshiped except You."[4]

There are several salutes to choose from which the Prophet has taught us. Each one adds a unique aspect to our prayer. Varying our salute with each prayer aids in better focus and concentration during these sacred moments.

---

[4] Transliterated: *"Subhanak Allahumma wa bihamdika wa tabarak kasmuka wata'la jaddukka wa la ilaha ghayruk."*

Expelling the intruder:

As you stand in Allah's hands, during such sacred moments, during such a grand encounter, no one is more envious of you now than Satan. So his mission is to steal every sweet moment you might have with The One you love, to steal every reward! So that you will finish your prayer, but only 1/3rd or 1/9th or 1/10th has been accepted, or 1/5th since the sobering reality of the matter is: *Only the parts of Salah you are mindful of are accepted by Allah.* [One will come on the Day of Judgment with over 90 years of Salah under his belt, but to his devastating surprise, only 6 years will have been recorded to his name, or 5, or 4.]

It is because of Satan that we begin to drift. Do you not notice that every worldly thought, matter, issue, predicament suddenly makes its way to your thoughts in Salah? Items you have lost for days or months are suddenly remembered and maybe even found! Even the designs on the prayer rug start to tell all sorts of entertaining stories! What do you do? You try to fight him and refocus. But he comes back. You fight him again. He comes back like a fly that will not leave you alone.

What is the solution for we are so weak!? We seek the help of our *Beloved* from the evils of His creatures. With *His Name* is barakah! [blessing] With *His Name* is total protection from all harm. Thus, before we proceed in our prayer any further, we formally express with confidence:

أَعُوذُ بِاللهِ مِنَ الشَّيطَانِ الرَّجِيمِ

"I seek Allah's protection from Satan the accursed".[5]

Feel its power as you say it!

The Essence and Heart of Salah

It was common that when the time for prayer came, the Prophet ﷺ would turn to Bilal [whose duty was to call out the Adhan – the call to prayer] and say, *"Relieve us with it, O Bilal"*. In other words, make the call, Bilal, for what will lighten our heavy burdens and will soothe and comfort us. For when the

---

[5] Transliterated: *"Aoothu billahi mina-shaitan arrajeem."*

Prophet was troubled with a difficult matter or much worry, he would turn to prayer. After all, doesn't Allah say: *"and seek [Allah's] help with patient perseverance and prayer"* [6]

Every people have their own method of seeking comfort, relaxation and escape. Some use music, some use exercises like Yoga, and some unfortunately-alcohol. But for us Muslims, we attain the benefits of all of the above and more, from Salah. We resort to the source of all solutions and the source of all peace and relief, *Our Beloved, Our Creator.*

Now we have guarded ourselves from Satan's ways and ready to enter upon the most sacred part of our Salah, the essence of it all...*The Fatihah!* The greatest Surah in the Quran! The segment of Salah without which you cannot have prayed and your prayer would be nullified. The segment where Allah actually answers back to us at every verse! How can we ever drift in this part of the prayer?

But first, let us remind ourselves. Again, what brought us to stand here right now? Oh yes, our endless love and deep longing to be with Allah. And when one meets up with his beloved, what is he first most likely to utter? It is the sweet sound of his Beloved's name! But this is no ordinary name. This is a name that blesses everything around it! Everything it falls upon! This is a name that lifts away any evil, harm and ache. With it we start, and with it we finish, and with it we taste the sweetness of this life and the sweetness of the next... *"Bismillah ar-Rahman ar-Raheem"* [In the name of Allah, The Most Gracious, The Most Merciful]. Feel it soothing your heart as it gently rolls off your lips. *"To Him [Allah] belong the most beautiful names.."* [7] And when you love someone, you savor in how *perfect* they are. Don't you? No one deserves this more than Allah. For only He, is truly perfect! *"Alhamdulillahi Rabbilalameen!"*

[All praise is due to Allah, The Cherisher and Sustainer of the Worlds!]. In praising Him, we are in essence establishing Allah's undeniable perfection. The Prophet ﷺ told us, *"Alhamdulillah* fills the scale!" Let gratitude fill our hearts when we utter it, He has blessed us with so much and always keep in mind that when we thank anyone in this world, we are in fact, thanking Allah Himself. He is the ultimate source, isn't He? Let's take it to another depth,

---

[6] Surah al-Baqarah 2:45.
[7] Surah al-Hashr 59:24.

when we say *"Alhamdulillah"*, we are even praising and thanking Allah for blessing us with *the ability to praise and thank Him*. As even this ability is from Him! So in reality, Allah establishes praise for Himself, through us. Glorified is He. Feel your dependence and need for Him, feel the healing effects of the gift of remembering and praising Him.

A Journey Beyond Our Limits

الْحَمْدُ لِلَّه رَبِّ الْعَالَمِينَ

"[All] praise is [due] to Allah, Lord of the worlds"[8]

So with *"Alhamdulillah"*, we have affirmed Allah's ultimate perfection and thanked Him for all that we are and *all that He is*. Now, most of us have received that Power Point email which zooms us out in powers of 10 from the cell world of a tiny plant leaf…all the way out to the planets, stars and galaxies that make up what lies beyond our planet earth, in this breathtaking universe! Now instead of starting out with that small leaf, start the zoom out process with the image of yourself as you stand before Allah in Salah. As you ponder over this image, think first of all of the physiological systems within your own body running in beautiful order to sustain you [blood system, immune system, nervous system, hormones, heart beats, respiration, firing neurons, skin cells, liver cells, spleen, kidneys, etc]. Move out now to what's around you. The marvels of our plant world, the animal world, the seven seas, the insect world, the microbial world. Further out to what surrounds you. The miraculous precision of the planets and our sun - our solar system, our galaxy. Further out still to the infinite star constellations, nebulas, galaxies. Now what about the world of the unseen? The world of the angels, the jinn and whatever life that lies out there that we have not been able to reach.

This may not be the end of it, but we have reached the limits of our knowledge, so start zooming back down. Back through all of that and back to where you were standing in prayer. Would you say you're just a speck in Allah's canvas above? Nowhere even close.....You are no longer even visible in relation to the magnificent size of Allah's universe! And imagine, this is just our heaven. The Quran tells us there are six more! And Allah presides above all of that!

---

[8] Transliterated: *"Alhamdu lillahi Rabbil alameen."*

11

And He is The One and Only, orchestrating the perfect order and function of it all!

How do you feel now as you stand before Him, praising Him and speaking to Him? How do you feel now being answered by Him as you recite every ayah? Do you still have it in you to defy some of His commands? Can you imagine yourself ever daring to commit another wrong against such Majesty and Might? Against such Omnipotence and such Sovereignty? How about *against such Love?* How much love must He have for us to select us out, given our insignificance in the canvas of His creation, for this beautiful exchange and these beautiful terms of endearment that are in Salah?

After all, He has blessed us with *the ability* to answer the call to prayer and stand before Him. That's an honor unlike any other! How can we not give our best? Can we ever turn our backs on prayer again knowing we are missing out on such a privilege!?

The Prophet ﷺ tries to help us understand the Grandeur before which we stand... He says ﷺ that the foot of Allah's Throne [al-Kursi] extends over the heavens and the earth.[9] And the seven heavens in comparison to Allah's Kursi, is like a small ring cast in the spans of a desert! And The Kursi, in comparison to the Throne itself, is a measure like it!

The next time you stand for prayer, view yourself from above and far away, so you can truly taste the meanings behind *"Rabbil Aalameen"* [Lord of the worlds!]

Unraveling More Secrets of al-Fatihah

الرَّحْمَنِ الرَّحِيمِ

"The Most Gracious, Most Merciful."[10]

Have you ever wondered why this comes before *"Maliki Yaumi-Deen"* [Master of the Day of Judgement] in al-Fatihah? Picture this scenario. You happened

---

[9] See al-Baqarah 2:255.
[10] Transliterated: *"Ar-Rahmanir Raheem."*

to be at the scene of a crime and there is an ongoing investigation. The trial begins and though you are innocent, the judge summons you for questioning.

He proceeds to question you in one of two manners: He at once bombards you with interrogation! [Why were you at the scene of the crime? What were you doing? At what time did you arrive? What did you see? etc.] When your heart nearly stops and your nerves can no longer stand it, the judge then reassures you, "by the way, we know you are innocent but we are collecting as much information as we can."

Or, he declares to you from the beginning that "we know you are innocent, but we appreciate all the information you can help us with", and then proceeds with his questions. You would be much more relaxed and comfortable in the second scenario, wouldn't you? So what does "ar-Rahmaan ar-Raheem" have to do with "Maliki Yaumi-Deen" and why does it come before it? To remind us that it is "ar-Rahmaan ar-Raheem" who will judge us on Judgment Day. These 2 names should kindle within us that sense of relief and reassurance in Salah when we are reminded of our stand before Allah on that terrifying day - Judgment Day. [Let us always strive to remain, worthy of this Mercy.]

"ar-Rahman ar-Raheem" declares that Allah's sovereignty is that of an all-encompassing Mercy [not Wrath]. In this life, He is there for everyone - believers and non-believers, the righteous and the wrongdoers. He feeds, clothes, heals, and provides, for all. He's not quick to punish but provides ample time for people to return to Him – a whole lifetime!

And Allah's Mercy is manifested either through His giving [of favours] or through His withholding of them. And when He sometimes withholds a favour from us, this in reality is the *heart of giving*, for we have been given of knowledge but so very little to immediately realize the wisdom. Again, it's a mercy in disguise!

"Does He Who created not know..?"[11] and Allah [swt] says "...But it may well be that you hate a thing the while it is good for you, and it may well be that

---

[11] Surah Mulk 67:14.

you love a thing the while it is bad for you, and Allah knows, whereas you do not know."[12]

When we say "ar-Rahmaan": this form of "Merciful" is in the Arabic form that implies *"to the fullest extent"*, like ghadbaan vs. ghaadeb [angry] or joo'aan vs. jaa'e' [hungry]. The former form implies the fullest extent of hunger and anger in comparison to the latter form. Thus Allah is truly the Most Merciful, to the fullest extent of the word!

In fact, "ar-Rahmaan" is the most *all encompassing* of His names. Just remember by which name He chose to preside over His Throne: *"ar-Rahmaan, above the Throne presides!"[13]* His most all-encompassing name is always coupled in the Quran, with his most all - encompassing creation - *His Throne*!

And this name only belongs to Him - You will never find anyone named "Ar-rahmaan", except Allah, but instead people will name "Abdur-Rahmaan" [the servant of the Most Merciful]. You will also never find anyone with the name *"Allah"* besides Allah. These two names are His, exclusively! Now "ar-Raheem" is the One who *delivers* His mercy to His creation. You will see this name used in the Quran when Allah speaks of His mercy to believers, specifically. If we knew well the true nature of Allah and the true nature of people, we would prefer without an instant of hesitation to deal with Allah, over having to deal with people. It suffices us to know that Allah's Mercy for us far exceeds the mercy of our own mothers for us. So *"Alhamdulillah"* for the kind of sovereignty He reigns by. Feel the rhythm of *ar-Rahmaan ar-Raheem* lift the heaviness off your heart.

A Little Shake-Up

مَالِكِ يَوْمِ الدِّينِ

"Master of the Day of Recompense"[14]

Why does Allah choose the word "Maalik" [Master, Lord, sovereign]? This is because any authority or power that was granted to creation in this life will be neutralized completely then! All dominion and power will now belong to the

---

[12] Surah al-Baqarah 2:216.
[13] Surah Taha 20:5.
[14] Transliterated: *"Maliki Yawmid deen."*

real *King!* In fact, no one can even utter a word or intercede for anyone else until He permits it. There are two recitations for this word: *Maaliki* [from ownership] and *Maliki* [from the sovereignty of a king] Two meanings to demonstrate Allah's sole and absolute control and authority on that dreaded day:

"On the Day you see it every nursing mother will be distracted from that [child] she was nursing, and every pregnant woman will abort her pregnancy, and you will see the people [appearing] intoxicated while they are not intoxicated; but the punishment of God is severe."[15]

يَوْمَ تَرَوْنَهَا تَذْهَلُ كُلُّ مُرْضِعَة عَمَّا أَرْضَعَتْ وَتَضَعُ كُلُّ ذَاتِ حَمْلٍ حَمْلَهَا وَتَرَى النَّاسَ سُكَارَى وَمَا هُمْ بِسُكَارَى وَلَكِنَّ عَذَابَ اللَّهِ شَدِيدٌ

"When man will flee from his own brother, and from his mother and his father, and from his spouse and his children."[16]

يَوْمَ يَفِرُّ الْمَرْءُ مِنْ أَخِيهِ وَأُمِّهِ وَأَبِيهِ وَصَاحِبَتِهِ وَبَنِيهِ

On that day, the heavens will be "rolled up like written scrolls!"[17] in "His Right Hand"[18] and the "trumpet will be sounded and all that are in the heavens and the earth will fall senseless…"[19] Who is left? The angel of the trumpet. So Allah Almighty takes his soul. Who is left? No one. And Our Lord calls, "To Whom does the dominion belong today?!" No answer. "To Whom does the dominion belong today?!" No answer. "To Whom does the dominion belong today?!" Dead silence. Allah finally answers Himself and declares, "To Allah, The One, The Overpowering!"[20]

---

[15] Surah al-Hajj 22:2.
[16] Surah Abasa 80:34-36.
[17] Surah al-Anbiyah 21:104.
[18] Surah az-Zumar 39:67.
[19] Surah az-Zumar 39:68.
[20] Surah al-Ghafir 40:16.

Then "a second [trumpet] is sounded, when, behold, they will stand and look on.."[21] And the "earth will shine bright with the light of its Lord!"[22] Your "Lord stands, and His angels, rank upon rank! And Hell, on that day, is brought face to face.."[23] And the sun draws near above the heads, on a day the length of which will be 50,000 years! How can we be saved from the horrors of that day? The answer, coming up next.

In the meantime, let's call upon these real images with *"Maaliki Yaumi-Deen"*. As you recite it in your prayer, pause upon it for a while. These words should not fall upon deaf ears and closed hearts, for a true Muslim's heart always oscillates between hope and fear. Hope for Allah's mercy and fear of Allah's displeasure and punishment.

The Key to Salvation

إِيَّاكَ نَعْبُدُ وَإِيَّاكَ نَسْتَعِينُ

"It is You we worship and You we ask for help."[24]

If we take the time to contemplate upon "Maliki Yaumi-Deen", it is a verse that should truly shake us! Many when they stand in prayer pay no attention to the words they utter. Those words never reach their hearts, but are an unconscious recitation of what they've memorized. "Will they not seek to understand this Quran or are there locks upon their hearts?"[25] It is said that those focused and whose hearts are truly humbled in prayer are like a fish in water, and those who are not…are like a bird in a cage. So what will save us from the horrors of that terrifying day? The answer lies in the next verse, for the next verse summarizes Surah al-Fatihah - The greatest Surah in the Book! And al-Fatihah summarizes the Quran! *"Iyyaka na'budu wa Iyyaka nasta'een"* [You alone we worship, and unto You alone we turn for help] Every Prophet gave his people this key to salvation, "I have come to you with a plain warning, that you worship none but Allah; for verily, I fear for you the punishment of a grievous day!"[26]

---

[21] Surah az-Zumar 39:68.

[22] Surah az-Zumar 39:69.

[23] Surah al-Fajr 89:22.

[24] Transliterated: *"Iyyaka na'budu wa iyyaka nasta'een."*

[25] Surah Muhammad 47:24.

[26] Surah Hud 11:26.

16

So what should be our ultimate goal in this life? To worship Allah and nothing else. For this is the reason we were created. And what are our means to attaining this goal? It is through seeking Allah's help. And what is the most important aspect of worship? It's sincerity of heart! That all that we are and all that we do is for Allah alone and no one else. To seek His pleasure only. Without that sincerity of intention, it would be as if you are a traveller journeying with bags of sand - carrying a heavy load, but a completely useless load! Make Allah alone your focus, not people, for what they think and say is irrelevant and cannot harm nor benefit you.

So if you were to be asked why you did what you did for any given deed/task, you can firmly answer 'for Allah!' and if asked 'Sure, and for what else?' You will affirm with certainty, "for nothing else!" "Shall we tell you who are the greatest losers in respect to their deeds? It is those whose labour has been wasted in this life while they thought they were doing good work..."[27]

Sincerity pure to Allah will change your life! The time has come to correct our intention in everything we do. The time has come to teach it to our children, so that every new thing they learn to do "is because *Allah* likes it!" and everything they are to refrain from doing "is because *Allah* doesn't like it!" To learn that their rewards are with Allah alone, not with people. Indeed however, pure sincerity of intention is not easy to attain, but it is not impossible either because we have been taught the magic words "wa Iyyaka nasta'een" [and unto You alone we turn for help].

If Allah helps you, there is nothing you cannot do. It is all in His hands. Ask and He will grant you. After all, doesn't He remind us that *you are all astray save for whom I guide!*[28] "Iyyaka na'budu wa Iyyaka nasta'een" was a verse over which those who came before us would weep for hours. One of them was once praying in Makkah, his friend went ahead and did the tawaf and when he returned to him, he was still at this verse, repeating it and crying, till the sun came up.. "Iyyaka na'budu wa Iyyaka nasta'een"...let us pause and reflect on it for a while, let it cleanse any hypocrisy that has ever tainted our hearts.

---

[27] Surah al-Kahf 18:103.
[28] Sahih Muslim

The Greatest Dua [supplication] You Can Ever Make

اهْدِنَا الصِّرَاطَ الْمُسْتَقِيمَ

"Guide us to the straight path"[29]

And now we come upon the greatest, wisest, most comprehensive Dua [supplication] we can ever make. If Allah guides us to the straight path, then He has helped us to worship Him like we should. [Recall the request for help that we made in the prior verse, "You alone we worship.. *and unto You alone we turn for help.*"]

If you notice, Surah al-Fatihah teaches us the proper etiquette of *how to ask* Allah when we have a need. It teaches us the proper way to make Dua so He will listen to us and answer. As befits a Majesty, we begin with the glorification and praise due to our Lord. Then we make our request. Now the path we need to win Allah's pleasure is called the Siraat - the straight path. But this path is not so easy to follow without assistance:

- There are specifics to this path that we will know, and specifics which we may not know [What is halal, what is haram. What is right, what is wrong.] In fact, the specifics we don't have enough knowledge of far outnumber the specifics we know enough about.

- And of these specifics we do know, there will be some we are physically able to carry out, and some we will not. [Like Hajj, Fasting, etc...]

- And of those requirements which we are physically able to carry out, at times we will enjoy them, and at times we may find them quite burdensome [Like waking up for Fajr prayer.]

- And even when we do accomplish that ordained duty, at times we fulfill the sincerity requirement, and at times we may not. And at times we may perform it properly according to the Prophetic example necessary for its acceptance, and at times, we may not.

---

[29] Transliterated: *"Ihdinas siratal mustaqeem."*

18

- And even if we fulfill all of the above: the knowledge, the ability, the right attitude, the sincerity, and the adherence to the Prophetic example, we will still need one more thing - *Steadfastness* - To perform it properly every time. Do you now see why we are so desperate for Allah's guidance to the straight path?

Do you see why we can't do it without His help? And do you now see how comprehensive this Dua is? Now as you know, there are 2 Siraats. One in this life: the one we spoke of above. The second one, is in the next life - described to be dangerously thin with a "sword's edge" sharpness! That is the one that spans over the fires of Hell, over which every one of us must pass if we are to reach Paradise.

"And there is none of you except he will come to it. This is upon your Lord an inevitability decreed. Then We will save those who feared Allah and leave the wrong-doers within it, on their knees." [30]

وَإِنْ مِنْكُمْ إِلَّا وَارِدُهَا كَانَ عَلَى رَبِّكَ حَتْمًا مَقْضِيًّا ثُمَّ نُنَجِّي الَّذِينَ اتَّقَوْا وَنَذَرُ الظَّالِمِينَ فِيهَا جِثِيًّا

If we are firm and steadfast on the first Siraat [the one in this life], then we will be firm on the second [in the next life]. So stability on the second is directly related to the degree of faith and good deeds earned in this life. Our strong faith and good deeds will be our guiding light on that dreadful bridge, amidst the darkness of Judgment Day.

"The day you shall see the believing men and the believing women, their light running forward before them and on their right.." [31] And so accordingly, some will cross it with the quickness of lightning! Some the speed of a shooting star! Some like the wind, some like a speeding stallion, some at running speed, while others will crawl on it with hands and knees, and others...will fall and never make it... And the Prophet will stand pleading in desperate prayer, *"My Lord, spare them. My Lord, save them…"* The Siraat of this life leads us to Allah. The Siraat of the next life leads us to Paradise. Do you now feel how serious this Dua is? *"Ihdina-Siraat Al-Mustaqeem"*- Our entire existence depends on it. The *"Ameen"* you'll pronounce now, after knowing the above, will be much more heartfelt, won't it? As a matter of fact, for any dua to be answered by Allah, the condi-

---

[30] Surah Maryam 19:71-72.
[31] Surah al-Hadeed 57:12.

tion is that it must come from a focused, attentive heart for *"Allah does not answer a supplication that comes from an absent/preoccupied heart."*

Concluding al-Fatihah

صِرَاطَ الَّذِينَ أَنْعَمْتَ عَلَيْهِمْ غَيْرِ الْمَغْضُوبِ عَلَيْهِمْ وَلَا الضَّالِّينَ

"The path of those upon whom You have bestowed favour,
not of those who have evoked [Your] anger or of those who
are astray."[32]

As we bid farewell to Surah al-Fatihah, we conclude with its last remaining verses. We talked about the Siraat and how we must strive, with Allah's help and guidance, to remain steadfast on this path in order to succeed in this life and the next. And since the right company makes all the difference in providing the support, reinforcement and good example to staying firm in faith and conduct, we specify that Allah guide us to *"the path of those on whom You bestowed Your Grace/blessings.."* [*Siraat-al-latheena an'amta alaihim*]

This is a reminder of all the good men/women that have succeeded before us. These are the Prophets, the righteous, the companions, and foremost - our Prophet Muhammad ﷺ. We are consoled when we remember them and the hardships they endured. It makes our trials bearable and we are relieved and comforted that insha'Allah we will be of their company in our next eternal life. "*Ghair-il-maghdhoobi alaihim*" [not of those whom upon them is wrath]. These are the people, who know very well the truth and what is right, but deliberately reject it and refuse to abide by it. So they have the knowledge but refuse to conform.

Example: Those who know they must pray, but choose not to. "*Wala-dhaalleen*" [nor of those who go astray]. These are the people who lack the knowledge of the truth and don't search for it, so they conform but to the wrong path.

Example: Those who pray, but in an unacceptable way. Did you notice that the words relating to Grace/Blessings are specific to Allah ["*an'amta*"- "*You*

---

[32] Transliterated: *"Ihdinas siratal mustaqeem.Siratal latheena an'amta alayhim.Ghayril maghdu-bi alayhim walad daalleen."*

bestowed"], while the words relating to wrath are not specific to Allah alone? This is because when it comes to granting favours and blessings, Allah is the sole provider of it all! But when evil is committed, this evokes the wrath of not only Allah, but the wrath of creation as well - The angels, the Prophets, the righteous, etc... And finally, *"Ameen"*. Ameen means "My Lord, grant/answer [my prayers]." With Ameen, we are pleading to the One whose in His hands is our guidance, success and salvation.

So express wholeheartedly, your need for Allah, just as if you have been sentenced to death and are pleading with the victim's family for pardon. There would be a desperation and passion to the tone of your voice, as your heart begs for their forgiveness. And here's another great reason for a wholehearted *"Ameen!"* The Prophet ﷺ tells us that if our *"Ameen"* coincides with the *"Ameen"* of the angels above, Allah will forgive all of our previous sins!

So this is no time to be drifting in our Salah, this is too good to miss! Our heart needs to be present and alive! As we mentioned earlier, Al-Fatihah is the heart of Salah and is one of its major pillars. The Prophet tells us, *"He has not prayed, the one who has not recited The Opening Chapter [al-Fatihah]."* As we have seen, it is the greatest Surah. In it we talk directly to Allah and He answers back to us at every verse. What does He say to us?

Listen to this: Allah said, "I have divided the prayer [al-Fatihah] into two halves between Myself and My servant, and My servant shall have what he asks for."

- If he says, "All praise and thanks be to Allah, the Lord of the worlds", Allah says, *"My servant has praised Me."*

- When the servant says, "The Most Gracious, the Most Merciful", Allah says, *"My servant has glorified Me."*

- When he says, "The Master of the Day of Judgment", Allah says, *"My servant has glorified Me"* or *"My servant has related all matters to Me."*

- When he says, "You [alone] we worship, and You [alone] we ask for help", Allah says, *"This is between Me and My servant, and My servant shall be granted what he sought"*.

- When he says, "Guide us to the straight path. The way of those on whom You have granted Your grace, not [the way] of those who earned Your anger, nor of those who went astray", Allah says, *"This is for My servant, and My servant shall be granted what he asked for."*

So the next time you are in prayer reciting al-Fatihah, remember to pause momentarily as the Prophet did after every verse, because His Majesty - with His beautiful face to yours, is responding to you... Feel it! What an honor it is to be *His* servant!

Recite with the Heart

We have now completed al-Fatihah and move on to the Quran recitation after it. Did you ever notice that any Quran recited in Salah is always recited when we are in the standing position? We do not recite al-Fatihah or any other Surah in the sitting position, nor during our Ruku [bowing], nor during our prostration. Why?

The standing position is man's most dignified, honorable and respectful position possible. And because this Quran speaks the most honorable and noble Speech, it is thus only befitting for the most noble Speech to be recited while in the most dignified and respectful of positions. The Prophet ﷺ tells us that he was prohibited from reciting the Quran while in Ruku [bowing] and while in Sujood [prostration]. The Quran is the Speech of Allah, The Most High, and is due our utmost respect. But how many a time have we recited it absent-mindedly, without any feeling or emotion, without any reflection on its powerful words? For many of us, if asked what of Allah's prohibitions did we just recite, we would have nó answer. What of Allah's commands did we just recite?

We cannot recall! People stand behind their Imam in prayer. He recites of Hell and Heaven, and they are off drifting of food and drink. If ever were we to conduct a historic interview with a powerful ruler, how attentive would we be? We would grant not only our submissive ears but all our hearts as well, wouldn't we? In fact, we would be so in tune that we'd probably even memorize this ruler's every word as he speaks! So how can we not be mindful of what we're reciting when it is Allah who speaks to us in this meeting? "Will they not seek to understand this Quran or are there locks upon their hearts?"[33]

 It is said that if our hearts were pure enough, we would never get enough of Allah's words! Remember, it is not in the *quantity* of Quran recited, but in the *quality* of how we recite and its effect on us. The Prophet once prayed an entire night with just one verse, repeating in tears: "If You should punish them- indeed they are Your servants, but if You forgive them - indeed it is You who is the Exalted in Might, the Wise.."[34]

So we are to recite with feeling, aware that we are talking to Allah and He is speaking to us. But how do we know what to feel with any given verse? Ibn al-Qayyim gave us basic guidelines to help us even if we lack thorough knowledge of tafseer. He says that:

- If a verse speaks of Allah's favours upon you, His names, His attributes… then it is *Love* that should fill your heart.

- If a verse speaks of Allah's mercy, forgiveness, the people of Heaven…then it is *Happiness, Comfort, and Hope* that should fill your heart.

- If a verse speaks of Allah's wrath, punishment, destroyed civilizations… then it is *Fear and Worry* that should fill the heart.

Thus we are always in a state between *Love, Hope and Fear* when reciting Allah's words. The Quran is greater than we know…

"If We had sent down this Qur'ān upon a mountain, you would have seen it humbled and coming apart from fear of God. And these examples We present to the people that perhaps they will give thought." [35]

لَوْ أَنزَلْنَا هَذَا الْقُرْآنَ عَلَى جَبَلٍ لَّرَأَيْتَهُ خَاشِعًا مُتَصَدِّعًا مِّنْ خَشْيَةِ اللَّهِ وَتِلْكَ الْأَمْثَالُ نَضْرِبُهَا لِلنَّاسِ لَعَلَّهُمْ يَتَفَكَّرُونَ

[33] Surah Muhammad 47:24.
[34] Surah al-Maidah 5:118.
[35] Surah al-Hashr 59:21.

Satisfy Your Greatest Need

We have now finished our recitation, we pause momentarily, then begin the bow as we simultaneously call out *"Allahu Akbar"* [Allah is Greater!] - A reminder to *refocus* should we have drifted, a reminder that…We stand here on earth in prayer, while Allah looks upon us from above the seven heavens. Our Salah should thus be a beautiful one, especially our bowing, for Allah is beautiful and loves that which is beautiful! We will not meet anyone this day, greater and more grand than Allah. So let us beautify and perfect this prayer to Him:

سُبْحَانَ رَبِّيَ الْعَظِيمِ

"How glorified and perfect My Lord is, The Supreme"[36]

Let the palms rest on the knees, fingers apart. Straighten the back and keep it level with the head. Maintain a calm hold till every part and joint is relaxed and has peacefully set in place. *"Subhana Rabbiyya Al-Adheem"*

Focus on the pronoun that means *"My"* [in Rabbi]. It adds that element of bonding, that ingredient for connection and love. He is *My* Lord [Rabbi] who has raised me in His care, clothing me, feeding me, healing me, nurturing me. A heartfelt *"Subhana"* meaning - far removed is He from any imperfection! *"Subhana Rabbiyya- Al-Adheem"* a second and third time as our hearts are humbled in submission before Him. Realize His Majesty, recall His sovereignty. I place all my hopes with *You, My Lord.*

Many of us perform this part of the prayer mechanically, devoid of any emotion or connection like that felt when reciting Quran or when down in prostration. But in reality, Ruku [bowing]' is an intense symbol of worship and servitude to our Lord! In it lies the essence of tremendous humbleness and humility! The Arabs back then knew this and the arrogant amongst them refused it in bold defiance! One companion requested, in his pledge to the Prophet, that he proceed from the standing position of prayer immediately to the Sujood [prostration] to bypass Ruku [bowing]' altogether!

Every one of us was created with particular needs, like the need to feel loved, the need to be alone for a while, the need to know that someone special awaits

---

[36] Transliterated: *"Subhana Rabbiyya- Al-Atheem"* [said 3 times or more].

you at home after a long hard day at work, the need to spend time with your children and kiss them to sleep, the need to hear good words, etc. When these needs go unsatisfied, an imbalance occurs within us that can affect the quality of our entire day. We might become irritable and cranky and not know why. A need within us has not been met that day.

But we have been created with a need far greater and more critical for our complete well-being than any other…It is the need *to worship*. To satisfy this need, people through the ages have worshiped everything under the sun [and including the sun]. They worshiped idols, water, animals, snakes, the sun, the stars, money, science, and even their own desires. And they exhaust great efforts and wealth to do so. Indeed, this need to worship must be satisfied, but none of the above can satisfy it like worshiping the One True God! And Salah fulfills that satisfaction with Ruku' [bowing] being an essential and critical part of it.

The Prophet and those before us used to feel such satisfaction and pleasure in Ruku [bowing] that they would hold in that position the same length as when in the standing segment of Salah. One companion said that he recited al-Fatihah, then al-Baqarah, ale-Imran, al-Nisa and al-Ma'idah and the companion Abdullah Ibn Zubair was beside him, still in his Ruku' [bowing]! Ibn Zubair was satiating his greatest need.

The Prophet ﷺ once saw a man rushing through his prayer, pecking up and down his Ruku [bowing] and Sujood [prostration]. He said, "*If this man dies [with his prayer] in this state, then he dies belonging to a creed other than the creed of Muhammad.*" Thus, our Ruku' [bowing] should be performed calmly, peacefully, according to the Prophet's example. This worldly life is full of hardships and aches. We laugh one day, only to cry the next. Its demands and toils leave us thirsty and tired.

What can quench this thirst better than prayer? The Prophet ﷺ said, "*The one who does not complete his Ruku [bowing]' properly, is like one who is starving and eats just a date or two. It does nothing to satisfy his hunger!*" Let us then, find our comfort and relief in our Ruku' [bowing] and Sujood [prostration] 17 times each day, we bow…Our love for Allah has to grow with that. And when you love Him, He will love you even more for He is the Most Kind, the Most Generous. And who can ever harm you…when the Creator Himself, loves *you*?

In Preparation for the Greatest Pillar of Salah

We just completed a beautiful station of Salah, the Ruku' [bowing]. The Ruku' [bowing] is the prelude to Sujood [prostration]...from one posture of submission, to a greater, more complete posture of submission! But before the Sujood [prostration], comes another beautiful station of Salah - and that is, the standing after the Ruku' [bowing]. The Prophet ﷺ said, *"Allah does not look to a servant's Salah if he does not straighten [upright] his back between his Ruku' [bowing] and Sujood [prostration]."* Therefore, that motionless, peaceful calm maintained in the other parts of Salah must be especially maintained here as well... allowing for the bones to return to their joints, for he also told us that *"The worst thief is the one who steals from his Salah"* [by rushing through it]. The Prophet ﷺ used to stand in this part of the prayer a length equal to that of his Ruku [bowing]'.

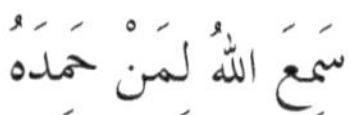

"May Allah answer he who praises Him"[37]

Yet as we rise for this stand, this time it is not "Allahu Akbar" that we call out, but instead, *"Sami'a-Allahu liman hamidah"*. Why? Remember what we said? That any dua/request made before The King is only proper and acceptable when preceded by praise and much extolling, right? Just as the Fatihah starts out with praise before the greatest dua is made [Ihdina-Sirat-Al-Mustaqeem], the same holds true here. For we are about to enter upon the greatest pillar of Salah the Sujood [prostration]!.. in which we will be the closest we can ever be to Allah! And during which, the duas/supplications, are always answered! *"Sami'a-Allahu liman hamidah"* therefore, signals us to praise Allah much before we are to make our duas when in Sujood [prostration]. And so what do we say upon that signal, once we have risen?

رَبَّنَا وَلَكَ الْحَمْدُ حَمْدًا كَثِيرًا طَيِّبًا مُبَارَكًا فِيهِ

We begin our praise: *"Rabbana walaka-alhamd "* [Our Lord, for You is all praise!]. We can add, *"hamdan katheeran tayyiban mubarakan feeh!"* [An abundant beautiful blessed praise!]. The Prophet was once leading in prayer. When he said *"Sami'a-Allahu-liman hamidah"*, one of the companions behind him added the above extension, *"hamdan katheeran tayyiban mubarakan feeh!"*. When the

---

[37] Transliterated: *"Sami'a-Allahu liman hamidah."*

prayer was finished, the Prophet ﷺ turned to his companions and asked, "Which one of you just said those words?" And the man replied "Me, ya Rasulallah." The Prophet commented, "I just saw thirty something angels racing to write it first!"

مِلْءَ السَّمَاوَاتِ وَمِلْءَ الأَرْضِ ، وَمِلْءَ مَا شِئْتَ مِنْ شَيْءٍ بَعْدُ

"[Praise] that fills/abounds the heavens, fills the earth, fills all that is between them, and fills all else of what You have willed [to be]!"[38]

We can go a step further and say the above dua. The "all else" implies the rest of creation that for us humans is beyond our imagination and grasp [Like the Throne, the Kursi, etc..] With those words, we are humbly admitting our limitations in knowledge in comparison to that of Our Creator.

This variety of sayings available to us helps us to regularly renew our focus in Salah, for better concentration. Let us praise and praise, and praise some more…We will never be able to praise Our Lord enough…For no one can ever praise Allah the complete praise justly due to Him, save for *one*…Do you know who that *one* is? It is Allah Himself! Only He can praise Himself the complete due praise! For there are attributes and qualities belonging to Allah that we cannot even imagine nor have they been revealed to us or to any other creation! Attributes, the knowledge of which lies with Him alone, a Magnificence completely beyond our scope!

Where True Happiness Really Lies

We have just finished the Ruku [bowing]' and the stand after it. This stand serves to prepare us for the greatest pillar of Salah! This pillar will be the sweet seal to the Rakah [unit of Salah]. All that came before it were merely leads to it. Preludes to the grand finale…The Sujood [prostration]! …What is Sujood [prostration] really about? Many of us have been performing the Sujood [prostration] robotically over the years, out of a mechanical routine, and thus have not felt its powerful effect. We will not be able to taste the true sweetness of any part of Salah until we get our *heart* into it! Sujood [prostration], as we have mentioned before, is the ultimate symbol of complete sub-

---

[38] Transliterated: *"Mil'a-Assamawaati wa mil'a-Al-Ard, wa mil'a ma bainahuma, wa mil'a ma-shi'ta min shay'en ba'd!"*

mission to our Creator…it is as if we are saying: "O Allah, what do You ask of me? I give You the most precious thing I own!..The most dignified and honored part of me…my face..and onto the lowest, most degraded spot around me, place it…the ground. For You alone, My Lord…I give You all that I am."

Sujood [prostration] is the real secret to true happiness. How? Ask yourself this: Where does Jannah [Paradise] lie - the place of ultimate bliss? *Up above* in the seventh heaven, *close to Allah.* Where does Hell lie - the place of ultimate misery? Down below, furthest from Allah, as the gateways of Heaven do not open up for the wrong-doers. What is the highest rank that can be reached in Jannah - the point of ultimate bliss? It is a place called "Al Firdous al-A'la", that's where the Prophet is! Its ceiling/upper limits is Allah's Throne! It is the highest place in Heaven, the closest one can ever come to Allah! In other words, for those who reside there, their neighbour is *Allah Himself!*

Let's keep asking…When the Prophet ﷺ was facing his toughest time in Makkah, feeling the deepest sadness, how did Allah console him and lift his spirits? He *raised* the Prophet *to Him* during the most momentous event of all time – al-Israa wal-Mi'raaj! Till he reached the closest a man can ever reach in nearness to his Lord! Even the things that are the source of happiness in this life- a good word, a good deed *rise* to Him where they belong for Allah says, *"Unto Him ascend all good words, and the righteous deed – He exalts/raises .." 39*

So, where does happiness lie? It lies *high above* with Allah. So the secret formula goes like this: the closer you become to Allah [*The King!*], the higher your spirits will rise, and thus the happier you will be! But how do we reach the levels of this great happiness? We must rise closer to that elevation. How do we do that? By lowering ourselves *down!* Recall the hadeeth.. *"He who humbles himself to Allah, Allah raises him."*- raises him in honour, raises him to the place of true happiness! And recall this hadeeth, *"The closest a servant ever is to His Lord, is when he is prostrating."* And what does Allah say at the end of Surah al-Alaq? *"..Prostrate and draw near [to Allah]"*

Do you realize now what you have been doing all these years? You were trying to draw nearer to Your Lord with every prostration. Your body is down firm to the ground, but your spirits are rising, trying to draw nearer to the Creator

---

39 Surah al-Fatir 35:10.

of the heavens and the earth! The Prophet ﷺ tells us, *"Perform much Sujood [prostration], for there is not a Muslim who performs a prostration but is raised by Allah a rank in Heaven, and disburdened of a sin."*...all the way till he reaches the highest ranks!..The highest Firdous - where Allah's Throne bounds it from above and in it abides, our beloved Prophet!

Need more proof? Rabi'a Ibn Ka'eb was once helping out the Prophet with water for his wudu' [ablution] when the Prophet said to him, "Ask me." Rabi'a replied, "I ask to be with you in Paradise." "Anything else?" The Prophet asked. "Only that", Rabi'a said. To that the Prophet replied, *"Then help me to help you [get there], by performing much Sujood [prostration]."* So you see now.. In order for your spirits to be lifted up higher and higher, you must bring your body down, lower. And just as your body does its Sujood [prostration], make sure *your heart* is in Sujood [prostration] as well...in prostration to The One, Who above the Throne is established, every day, directing new affairs.. To Him rise the needs and deeds of everyone. Everyone needs Him and He needs no one - Forgiving a sin here, easing a difficulty there. Strengthening someone weak, mending a broken heart.

Bringing into life, taking a life. Guiding to Him whom He wills, leading astray whom He wills. Providing for and blessing a people, taking away a blessing from another. Honoring a people, degrading and humiliating another. Bringing joy and happiness to some, taking it away from others. When your heart performs a prostration, you will know it. For you will rise from it with a special *glow*, "On their faces is their sign from the effect of their prostration.."[40]

It is that sign of the grace and light of Allah - that gentleness and kindness, that blessed peace and calmness that can come from no other source. Sujood [prostration] is the most special part of prayer. Sujood [prostration] is very precious! How many a worry has Sujood [prostration] relieved. How many a difficulty and trial has Sujood [prostration] resolved. How many a need has Sujood [prostration] fulfilled. How many a dua went unanswered, till it was made...in Sujood [prostration]!

Bring yourself down to the ground, to bring yourself closer to The Lord. Prostrate with body, heart and soul.. and taste the sweetest feeling in the world....Taste the real happiness of this world!

---

[40] Surah al-Fath 48:29.

The Perfect Sujood

We continue with the greatest pillar of Salah, the Sujood [prostration]! Now don't you wish you could have watched the Prophet himself as he did his Sujood [prostration]? This is the aim of today's segment, to carry to you the description of the proper Sujood [prostration], just the way our Messener prostrated before Allah, in hope that we can perfect our own performance of this precious pillar. When you are ready to perform the prostration, make sure to call out "Allahu Akbar" *on your way down* for Sujood [prostration]....Not before, nor after, but during the descent. The stronger opinion is that the palms are to touch the ground first before the knees, to avoid resembling the descent of a beast [camel].

Next, the head makes a gentle contact with the ground till the forehead [and nose] is firm upon the ground. Ensure that there is no barrier [as that of a head covering] that might prevent direct contact of your forehead with the place of prostration. With palms firmly down, keep fingers close together. Point fingers, knees and toes towards the Qiblah. Palms can either be parallel with the head, or parallel with the shoulders.

Keep the elbows elevated off the ground. [For men] extend elbows as far away from your sides as possible. Keep abdomen away from the thighs. The Sujood [prostration] is done on a total of 7 body parts: The forehead [including the nose], the two palms, the two knees, and the two feet [toes]....All firm upon the ground till every bone and joint is fixed in place with peace and calm. The Prophet ﷺ never recited Quran in this position, but instead, he made much dua. He said, *"The closest a servant ever is to His Lord, is when he is prostrating so make in it much dua."* And what have we been taught to say, when we are down so low -

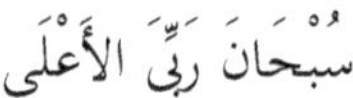

"How glorified and perfect My Lord is, The Most High!"[41]

---

[41] Transliterated: *"Subhana Rabbiyal-A'ala"* [said 3 times or more]

We can add,

سُبْحَانَكَ اللَّهُمَّ رَبَّنَا وَبِحَمْدِكَ ، اللَّهُمَّ اغْفِرْ لِي

"How perfect You are O Allah, Our Lord, and I praise You.
O Allah, forgive me."[42]

Or,

سُبُّوحٌ قُدُّوسٌ رَبُّ الْمَلَائِكَةِ وَالرُّوحِ

"Perfect and Holy [is He], Lord of the Angels
and Ruh [i.e. Angel Jibrael]."[43]

The Prophet taught us many supplications, each with a different meaning, each with a unique flavor. Each serves to renew our focus.

To make dua is to *talk* to Allah. When you love someone, you love to talk to him more. You love to stay engaged longer! Do you remember when Allah spoke to Prophet Musa in the valley of Tuwa [below Mount Sinai]?[44] As Allah spoke to him, Musa listened and listened, so absorbed! Then, what did he do when Allah suddenly asked him, *"And what is that in your right hand, O Musa?"* Musa was feeling such a comfort and pleasure as he engaged with the words of his beloved Lord that a euphoria enveloped his answer… and with that… he set off in speech!… *"It is my staff; I lean upon it; and I bring down leaves with it for my sheep.."* He was so lost in the rapture of this special engagement… till he remembered the Grandeur before Him, and so…cut it short, *".. and in it I have other uses."*

So as you prostrate in nearness to Him, try to feel the pleasure Prophet Musa felt. Remember the love you hold for Him. Talk to Him, praise Him, ask Him, unload your burdens at His door, and reach out for the peace that only He can bring.

---

[42] Transliterated: *"Subhanak-Allahumma Rabbana wa bi-hamdik. Allahumma ighfirli."*
[43] Transliterated: *"Subboohun Quddoosun, Rabbul-mala'ikati wa-rruuh"*
[44] See Surah Taha 20:11-47.

اللَّهُمَّ إِنِّي أَعُوذُ بِرِضَاكَ مِنْ سَخَطِكَ ، وَبِمُعَافَاتِكَ مِنْ عُقُوبَتِكَ ، وَأَعُوذُ بِكَ مِنْكَ ، لاَ أُحْصِي
ثَنَاءً عَلَيْكَ أَنْتَ كَمَا أَثْنَيْتَ عَلَى نَفْسِكَ

"O Allah, I seek refuge within Your pleasure, from Your displeasure. And within Your pardon, from Your punishment. And I seek refuge in You, from You. I cannot enumerate Your praise. You are as You have praised Yourself."[45]

We have one Ruku [bowing] in each unit of Salah, but two prostrations, why? Because the Sujood [prostration] is the Salah's greatest pillar, it is performed twice! Once is just not enough. The Prophet ﷺ used to lengthen his prostrations, savoring in these precious moments with Allah. [This was an especially precious time for his young grandchildren as well! And he would not come up from his Sujood [prostration], till their riding fun was satisfied!]

A Desperate Plea!

As we have seen so far, every station in Salah has a special meaning and a unique significance, so that with every position we move to, we are transported into a new and different scene. These transitions help our *minds* to stay aware of and internalize the words we utter. These transitions help our *hearts* to stay alive throughout our Salah - alive with alternating feelings and emotions before Allah: Those of love, hope, fear, and humility. The station we arrive at now is one which should inspire immense humility and fear. It is a position resembling a position occurring on Judgment Day:

"And you will see every nation kneeling [from fear]. Every nation will be called to its record [and told], "Today you will be recompensed for what you used to do. This, Our record, speaks about you in truth. Indeed, We were having transcribed whatever you used to do." [46]

وَتَرَى كُلَّ أُمَّةٍ جَاثِيَةً كُلُّ أُمَّةٍ تُدْعَى إِلَى كِتَابِهَا الْيَوْمَ تُجْزَوْنَ مَا كُنْتُمْ تَعْمَلُونَ هَذَا كِتَابُنَا يَنْطِقُ عَلَيْكُم بِالْحَقِّ إِنَّا كُنَّا نَسْتَنْسِخُ مَا كُنْتُمْ تَعْمَلُونَ

In our present world, it is that mortifying position of one about to hear out his death sentence… A position of someone in utmost desperation for a pardon, a savior… It is the sitting between the 2 prostrations.. down on your knees! What is it that we are to say when in this position? No words can we possibly need more, than: رَبِّ اغْفِرْ لِي رَبِّ اغْفِرْ لِي "*Rabbi ighfirli Rabbi ighfirli*" [My Lord forgive me! My Lord forgive me!] Twice, three times, four times, or more. How many times have we wronged ourselves and transgressed Allah's bounds?

It is a time to ask for much forgiveness as we sit in this position of full servitude and helplessness. The Prophet ﷺ used to sit in this position a length equal to that of his Sujood [prostration], seeking Allah's forgiveness and making the following dua:

اللَّهُمَّ اغْفِرْ لِي، وَارْحَمْنِي، وَاهْدِنِي، وَاجْبُرْنِي، وَعَافِنِي، وارْزُقْنِي، وَارْفَعْنِي

"O Allah forgive me and have mercy on me, guide me and enrich me,
give me health and provide for me and raise me in rank."[47]

The provision we ask of Allah, implies a provision in this life, and more importantly, in the next. On Judgment Day, as creation fretfully awaits its judgment, the Prophet ﷺ will prostrate before Allah's Throne in a prolonged Sujood [prostration] - praising, glorifying, praying and crying - crying for the people of his nation....Till Allah answers him, "*Lift your head up, O Muhammad. Ask and it will be granted, intercede and it will be accepted.*"

The Prophet will rise from his Sujood [prostration] to this position, and begin his intercession for us. From this we can understand, that our prayers can be answered both when we are in Sujood [prostration], or after. As we beg for Allah's forgiveness, we proceed to make another Sujood [prostration], for we need to draw closer still, to Our Lord...One Sujood [prostration] is not enough. And as the first Surah of the Quran, Surah al-Alaq, starts out with a recitation ["*Read!*"] and ends with a prostration, so is the case with the Rakah [unit] of Salah - It starts with recitation and ends with prostration.. Every act of worship has a special beauty to it, a unique flavor. The more we learn the

---

[47] Transliterated: "*Allahumma ighfirli wa-rhamni, wa ihdini wa-jburni, wa aafini wa-rzuqni wa-rfa'ni.*"

33

more we can taste that flavor and feel that beauty, after all: "Are they equal- Those who know and those who do not know?"[48]

The Farewell Scene

التَّحِيَّاتُ لِلَّه وَالصَّلَوَاتُ وَالطَّيِّبَاتُ ، السَّلاَمُ عَلَيْكَ أَيُّهَا النَّبِيُّ وَرَحْمَةُ اللهِ وَبَرَكَاتُهُ ، السَّلاَمُ عَلَيْنَا وَعَلَى عِبَادِ اللهِ الصَّالِحِينَ ، أَشْهَدُ أَنْ لاَ إِلَهَ إِلاَّ اللهُ وَأَشْهَدُ أَنَّ مُحَمَّدًا عَبْدُهُ وَرَسُولُهُ

'Words of Praise and Salutations are for Allah, and Prayers and pure words. Peace and salutations upon you O Prophet and the Mercy of Allah and His Blessings. And peace be upon us and upon all of Allah's righteous servants. I testify that none has the right to be worshipped except Allah, and testify that Muhammad is His Slave and Messenger.'[49]

If you have just finished the first Rakah [unit] of your Salah, then rise for the second and rise for a new chance to improve your focus and to ensure that this time, your heart and mind are fully alive with the humbleness and humility required of us in Salah. If this is your last Rakah, then we have arrived at the Farewell Scene… the sweet ending to this beautiful meeting between a servant and his Merciful Lord. We have arrived at…The Tashahhud.

Our hands are to be placed upon our knees or just above - on the lower thighs. As is proper when speaking to Our Lord, our farewell address must also begin first, by sending all praise and glorification to Allah, for His eternal existence, His perfection, and His sovereignty….Greet Him directly; speak to Him with these beautiful words: *"Attahiyyatu lillahi"*. All *"Attahiyyat"* [greetings/praises/glorification] is due to Allah alone and no one else. *"Wassalawatu"*- and all our duas and prayers are to Him. *"Wattayyibat"*- and all the good deeds, in the form of actions or words, are for Him alone. For Allah accepts only what is good, pure, and sincere.

Now the words you will pronounce next will travel off to another land…thousands of kilometers away.. to Madinah!.. to where rests the blessed body of the greatest man who ever lived - our beloved Prophet, *"Assalamu*

---

[48] Surah az-Zumar 39:9.

[49] Transliterated: *"At-tahiyyatu lillahi was-salawatu wat-tayyibat. Assalamu alayka ayyahun nabiyyu wa rahmatul-lahi wa barakatahuh.Assalamu alayna wa ala ibadillahis saliheen.Ashhadu alla ilaha ilal-ha wa ashadu anna Muhammadan abduhu wa rasuluh.'*

alaika ayyuha-nnabiyyu warahmatullahi wabarakatuh"- May the peace, mercy and blessings of Allah be upon you, O Prophet! Everyday, you send this special greeting to him and he answers you back! Listen to this hadeeth: The Prophet ﷺ said, *"There is not one who sends upon me his peace and blessings but Allah returns my soul to me, so that I can return upon him, my peace and blessings."*

Please glance over at the nearest doorway to you and imagine that the Prophet ﷺ has just entered through that door. With his beautiful radiant face touched with a hint of rose, with his neatly wrapped 'amama [head cover], in his pure white sweet-scented clothes.. and with his warm smile that melts your heart. He has chosen to greet only one today, and that's you! How would you feel? What would you say? With these loving words above, you are speaking directly to the Prophet now. And just think.

You have this honorable privilege at least 5 times everyday! How many of us have wished to have lived during his time, to see him and to be with him... With these words above, we *are* with him! So let us greet our Prophet with a heart full of affection and full of appreciation and gratitude for the best example he has set and for this priceless message he has brought to us. And while we reflect over how much love and esteem we hold for him, let us remember...that we are now sitting in the hands of The One who created our Prophet and how much love we hold for Allah Himself - Whom as a result of your greetings and peace upon His Prophet, now sends upon *you* a ten-fold share of the blessings and peace!

After sending off praise and greetings upon Allah, then upon His Prophet, we now send the blessings of peace upon ourselves and upon all of Allah's righteous servants: *"Assalamu alaina wa ala ibadillahi-saaliheen"*- upon every righteous servant whether in the heavens or earth - angel or man. Next- those powerful words of Tawheed- those words that affirm and renew our faith and sincerity: *"Ashhadu anna la ilaha illa-llah, wa ashhadu anna Muhammadan abduhu wa rasuluh"*- I bear witness that none has the right to be worshiped except Allah, and I bear witness that Muhammad is His servant and messenger. When death comes upon us, there is not one of us, but he will die sometime between any two given times of Salah - either between Fajr and Dhuhr, or Dhuhr and Asr, or Asr and Maghrib, etc.

The Prophet ﷺ tells us, *"The one whose last words [in this life] are "La ilaha illallah", enters Paradise."* This is no time to drift! These words of affirmation above are the key to paradise! Finally, as this beautiful meeting nears its end, Allah has guaranteed that in these last precious moments you have with Him, your duas made here - are answered! So first, ask for Allah's prayers and blessings upon our beloved Prophet and his family, seek much forgiveness for yourself and for your parents, then ask The Most-Gracious, Most-Merciful the best of this life and the best of the next. Try to learn the prayers [duas] that the Prophet ﷺ used to say, as they cover every possible need we could ever have.

اللَّهُمَّ صَلِّ عَلَى مُحَمَّدٍ وَعَلَى آلِ مُحَمَّدٍ كَمَا صَلَّيْتَ عَلَى إِبْرَاهِيمَ وَعَلَى آلِ إِبْرَاهِيمَ إِنَّكَ حَمِيدٌ مَجِيدٌ ، اللَّهُمَّ بَارِكْ عَلَى مُحَمَّدٍ وَعَلَى آلِ مُحَمَّدٍ كَمَا بَارَكْتَ عَلَى إِبْرَاهِيمَ وَعَلَى آلِ إِبْرَاهِيمَ إِنَّكَ حَمِيدٌ مَجِيدٌ

"O Lord, bless Muhammad and his family as You blessed Ibrahim and his family. You are the Most-Praised, The Most Glorious. O Lord, bestow Your grace on Muhammad and his family as You bestowed it on Ibrahim and his family. You are the Most-Praised, the Most-Glorious".[50]

As you end your prayer and turn your head to the right in Salam upon those with you, you should be feeling a deep sense of comfort, peace and serenity now. If you don't, then your deeds are to blame, as they weigh down and numb the heart.. and distance you from your Lord. Seek Allah's forgiveness for the deficiency in your Salah at least 3 times upon its completion, and stand up for Sunnah prayer - for another chance to attain that needed peace that only Allah can supply. And always remember, as your love for Allah grows and grows and as you draw nearer to Him, your heart will begin to come alive with the due humbleness before Him, your focus will improve, and finally, you will be able to taste the true beauty of Salah!

---

[50] Transliterated: *"Allahumm salli 'ala Muhammad wa 'ala ali Muhammad kama sallayta ala Ibraheem wa 'ala ali Ibraheem innaka hameedun majeed. Allahumma barik 'ala Muhammad wa 'ala Muhammad kama barakta 'ala Ibraheem wa 'ala ali Ibraheem innaka hameedun majeed"*

A Meeting Announcement - The Call to Prayer

We're not quite done yet. A few words about Adhan [the call to prayer]. Do you know when Salah really starts? Would you say at "Allahu Akbar"? Actually, it starts way before then. It starts with the *Adhan!* The Prophet says, *"Each one of you is [really] in a state of prayer as he awaits [to perform] the Salah."* Adhan signals you to prepare yourself for your upcoming meeting with Allah [Salah]. It should summon those feelings of humbleness and humility felt when reminded of Allah. Thus, you are already in Salah because you are now in that Salah mindset! Adhan also expels Satan, since upon hearing it, he flees with anger and rage!

Knowing this fact - that he's no longer there to distract you, should improve your concentration in prayer and help you attain that needed level of humbleness and humility for a beautiful satisfying prayer. Adhan is your chance to augment your Salah rewards that might have been reduced due to deficiencies you could not prevent [i.e. when you drift.] So how do we augment that reward? The Prophet tells us that the Muadhin [the one who makes the call to prayer] gets the reward of everyone who prays with him. So, for example, if 100 men pray with him, he gets the rewards of these 100 prayers. For us to accumulate a reward similar to this Muadhin, all we need to do… is repeat the Adhan after him! *"Say as they [the Mudhins] say"*- was our Prophet's tip! So imagine if you were repeating the Adhan in Makkah, where millions pray, and where one Salah equals 100,000 in worth!

Imagine your rewards then! Such is Allah's grace and generosity. A small simple act, met in return, with such immense rewards! What does the Adhan start with? *"Allahu Akbar!"*- Allah is Greater! No one is more important in your life right now than He! Leave your business, leave your job, leave your family and your children, leave your sleep! Allah is Greater than all of it - It's time to report to Him now. This is why the Muadthin repeats these words more than once.

And for what are we to rise and leave all of that? The answer lies in the words that come next: *"La ilaha ill Allah"*- There is no one worthy of worship except Allah! For you alone O Allah, I leave it all behind. Stated another way - to ignore the call and neglect a prayer is to say that what is at hand is more important than Allah - that it is more worthy of worship than He. What comes after "La ilaha ill Allah"? Well when we rise to pray, whose example do we follow in the way we pray? It's the Prophet's example, *"Pray as you have seen me pray."* Thus the Adhan calls out, *"Ashhadu anna Muhammadan Rasulullah"*- I testify that Muhammad is Allah's messenger. So this establishes that for any given deed, two criteria must be met before a deed can be accepted: *Sincerity* to Allah [La ilaha illAllah] and *Conformance* to His Prophet's example [Ashhadu anna Muhammadan Rasulullah].

This fundamental rule is summarized in the last verse of Surah al-Kahf:

Say, "I am only a man like you, to whom has been revealed that your god is one God. So whoever would hope for the meeting with his Lord - let him do righteous work and not associate in the worship of his Lord anyone." [51]

قُلْ إِنَّمَا أَنَا بَشَرٌ مِثْلُكُمْ يُوحَى إِلَيَّ أَنَّمَا إِلَهُكُمْ إِلَهٌ وَاحِدٌ فَمَنْ كَانَ يَرْجُو لِقَاءَ رَبِّهِ فَلْيَعْمَلْ عَمَلًا صَالِحًا وَلَا يُشْرِكْ بِعِبَادَةِ رَبِّهِ أَحَدًا

Realize how honorable our Prophet Muhammad is...No individual's name is raised as high as his. With Muslims living in every part of the globe, calling out their Adhan as the sun shines upon their land, the entire planet glorifies Muhammad ﷺ around the clock - minute by minute, uninterrupted, 24 hours a day! So join the greatest glorification campaign ever known! Repeat after your Muadhin! So what is required of us now, after we have testified to sincerity and conformance? *"Hayya 'ala-Salah!"* [Come/Rise to prayer!]. But instead of repeating these words now, what must we say? We are to say *"La hawla wala quwwata illa billah"*- There is no might or power [in me] but which Allah [grants me]. Only Allah can help me rise in obedience and facilitate my worship. I can't do it without His help. So Adhan is similar to the expressions of the Fatihah where we first establish that worship is due to Him alone [*iyyaka na'budu*], then we seek His help to carry it out [*wa iyyaka nasta'een*]

The next words should inspire in us sheer joy and enthusiasm! The next words promise us all the success - *"Hayya 'alal-Falaah!"*- [Come/Rise to success!] If this Salah guarantees my success in my work in this life and then in the next, then how can I not rise and answer its call? And again, the power I have in me comes only from Allah so to these words I say again, *"La hawla wala quwwata illa billah."* And finally, the words that end the Adhan are similar

---

[51] Surah al-Kahf 18:110.

to those that started it- *"La ilaha illAllah"*. Where "Allahu-Akbar" in the beginning calls upon you to leave the Dunya [this world] because Allah is Greater - Now "la ilaha illAllah" summons you to come focus upon the Akhira [the next life], the real life to work for.

The next time you hear the Adhan, hear it as the long awaited announcement that your meeting with your loved One is almost here! Listen to it like a child would as he stands in the arrivals terminal anxiously awaiting his mother's return, and then hears the announcement, that her flight has just touched down! The Adhan also has its unique flavor, for *"whomever loves to meet/be with his Lord - his Lord also loves to meet/be with him.."*

And this longing and yearning to be with Allah should inspire you to rush to your Salah without delay, just as Prophet Musa rushed to His Lord, *"..and I hastened to You, my Lord, that You may be pleased [with me]."*[52]

The sad reality today is that Adhan has become for many, a dull play of words that fades unnoticed into the backdrop of the commotion of busy hectic lives. But as we learn of what its words really signify, we come to realize the power of Adhan in retuning our outlook on life and on our entire existence.

Fit To Be Seen

A few words about Wudu' [Ablution]…Many of us perform our Wudu' simply out of habit, assuming that there is nothing really special about it other than that it is required before we can make our Salah. But there is so much more to Wudu' than we know...You probably already know *how* to perform Wudu', what you're to say while doing it, how the Prophet ﷺ did it, and things such as not wasting water, etc. What else could there be to it? Well, notice that the above are all actions of your faculties – your hands, mouth, feet. But where is the *heart?* Isn't the heart the place where the intention lies? How many a small act, augmented in the scales because of the niyyah [intention] and how many a great act, reduced in the scales also because of… the niyyah! [intention]

Thus, when we involve the heart, we add to the weight of a given action, far

---

surpassing the amount of rewards earned by just the faculties alone. So the next time you rise to go wash up for Salah, don't just fulfill a prescribed requirement before Salah but add on the following intentions to gain much much more: Rise with the intent of wholehearted obedience.. Obedience to Allah as you fulfil His commands of ayah 6 of Surah al-Ma'idah, "O you who have believed, when you rise to [perform] prayer, wash your faces and your forearms to the elbows and wipe over your heads and wash your feet to the ankles."

Rise with the intent of complete *conformance* to our beloved Prophet's example- the best example. Rise with the intent of *cleansing* yourself of your wrong deeds. Since wudu' is your prerequisite before entering upon Allah and no one is permitted to enter upon Him except in a state of purity, wudu' cleanses you from the outside till you can be cleansed next- from the inside! Our Prophet said, *"He who performs wudu' and perfects it, his wrong deeds leave his body till it runs off with the last drop of water [he's cleansed completely]!"* or *"till it runs off even from under his nails!"*

And these sins are washed off from every body part of wudu'- the sins committed by his hands, his feet, his face [eyes, mouth/tongue]. Try to visualize this purification as the water washes it all away. Visualize it with a heart full of hope in Allah's mercy. Upon completion, proclaim the Shahadah

أَشْهَدُ أَنْ لا إِلَهَ إلاّ اللهُ وَحْدَهُ لا شَرِيكَ لَهُ وَأَشْهَدُ أَنَّ مُحَمَّداً عَبْدُهُ وَرَسُولُهُ

"I bear witness that none has the right to be worshipped except Allah, alone without partner, and I bear witness that Muhammad is His slave and Messenger."[53]

and then say,

اللّهُمَّ اجْعَلْنِي مِنَ التَّوَّابِينَ وَاجْعَلْنِي مِنَ الْمُتَطَهِّرِينَ

"O Allah, make me of those who return to You often in
repentance and make me of those who remain clean and pure."[54]

O Allah, make me of those who return to You often in repentance, and make me of those who remain clean and pure!

---

[53] Transliterated: *"Ashhadu an la ilaha illal-lahu wahdahu la shareeka lah, wa-ashhadu anna Muhammadan Aabduhu warasooluh."*

[54] Transliterated: *"Allahumma ij'alni mina-Tawwabeen, waj'alni minal Mutatahhireen."*

With wudu', you are preparing for the meeting with The King and as before any meeting of such status and prestige, one needs to beautify himself- going to great lengths to appear presentable! Wudu' gives you all that beautification and that "fit to be seen" appearance before the Lord. This beauty given by wudu' will stay with us till the Day of Judgment. The Prophet ﷺ once said, *"How I wish we could have seen our brothers.."*- Those of his nation who had yet to come after him. That's us!

He will be able to identify us on that day, from the bright traces of our wudu'- in our faces and our extremities! The Prophet encourages us to wash even beyond the required point on each body part - beyond the elbows and the ankles- for an even brighter more luminous effect, on that day! This extra effort not only erases sins, but also raises the ranks! Wudu' can eventually take us even higher and higher in rank- to a status unimaginable! How? The Prophet one morning asked Bilal, *"How did you get ahead of me in Jannah?* [meaning- as a servant walks ahead of his master in serving him] *I entered Jannah and heard your movement before me!"* Bilal answered, "Well ya Rasulullah, Never did I make the Adhan but prayed two Rakahs after it, and never did I lose my wudu' but [immediately] renewed it." *"With that!"*, commended our Prophet. When we finish our wudu', we seal it with the Shahadah - *"Ashhadu anna la ilaha illallah, wa ashhadu anna Muhammadan Rasulullah."*... upon which all the 8 gates of Heaven open up — for us to enter through any gate we choose!

In Summary

It was said that when the time for prayer came, Ali would shake and his face would go pale and he would say, "The time has come to keep the trust that was offered to the heavens and the earth and the mountains but they declined to bear it and that I [man, foolishly] undertook to bear it.." [in reference to ayat 33:72]. The "trust" is the *responsibility of free will* - the responsibility to choose between good and evil.

When we die, Salah is the first responsibility we will be judged for, if it is sound [accepted], then all our deeds after it will be sound [accepted].. and if it is corrupt [unaccepted], then all our deeds after it will be corrupt [unaccepted]. The Prophet ﷺ said, *"whoever abandons it [prayer], has disbelieved ["kufr"]!"*

It is not only Salah's obligatory aspect, however, that should compel us to tend to it. This would be an incomplete intention. Consider this example- People originally used to eat to survive, right? No longer so in today's world where people now survive to eat! Eating nowadays has become an art form- with colorful varieties to tempt the eye, multiple course meals, and delectable desserts afterwards. To savor each and every bite, to gain that pleasure- Such should be the case for Salah. Go to it because you love it and because you yearn for the pleasure you find in it!

Prepare ahead for it. Just as a nice meal starts out with a tasty appetizer before the scrumptious main course, start your preparation for Salah with the sounding of the Adhan. Wash up again even if you still have your wudu'- give yourself more light!

Start asking yourself, "What am I about to do now? Who am I about to meet?", and don't just cover up your 'awra with any old clothes, but make extra effort to beautify yourself for The King - change into something beautiful and presentable. Turn off your phone, choose an undecorated prayer rug, face the qibla, straighten your lines if in congregation, and aim to pray in the first row for better concentration.

This is Salah - the most beautiful way to worship! An act that brings such a satisfying comfort, a true quenching of that spiritual thirst! Your body maybe on earth, but your soul is floating around The Most Merciful's Throne! Salah is Allah's greatest gift to us. In it is the peace and true happiness that we all yearn and search for. This life is full of hardship, trials, and aches. We need to rid ourselves of these aches. We need relief from it all and who possesses this ultimate relief? No one but Allah. And this relief we will find in Salah. *"O you who have believed, seek help through patience and prayer. Indeed, Allah is with the patient"* [55]

Remember what the Prophet ﷺ would say when he was heavily burdened with a matter and the time for prayer came: *"Relieve us with it, O Bilal.."* This comfort - this true peace and pleasure is attainable not just by the great men and women who came before us, but by anyone who can unlock the secrets of Salah as they did. The secrets for reaching these levels of peace, pleasure and

---

[55] Surah al-Baqarah 2:153.

relaxation does not only lie in better focus and concentration, but in depths far greater:

Ensure the Presence of the Heart - Your heart must be in it if you want to feel the effects. This is not at all difficult to achieve. All you need is 10 minutes to focus on the love you hold for Allah. Forget this world for now... there's more than 23 hours for that! Devote these 10 minutes now to Allah and to the peace and pleasure that comes from being with Him.

Comprehend the Words and Actions of Salah - When you are aware of what you are saying and doing then you remain focused. Since Allah ordained Salah for us then this *is* achievable. Did you know, that you are only rewarded for the parts of Salah that you are aware and cognizant of? So if we can stay focused throughout a 2-hour movie or an exam, for sure we can stay focused now. Everything in this world worships Allah around the clock, surely we can do 10 minutes. Just seek Allah's help and you will reach a point where you'd wish Salah never ended!

Come to Salah with a feeling of **Hope** [*Rajaa*]- Hope is a deeper emotion that must be present when you pray. The more you know about Allah, the more your heart can feel this hope - hope for His Mercy, for His forgiveness, His acceptance, His love, His closeness. Note that "hope" is different from "wish". Hope is coupled with action - where you work for what you hope for. So hope for Allah's Mercy and ask Him for it,

"Call upon Me; I will answer you."[56]

وَقَالَ رَبُّكُمُ ادْعُونِي أَسْتَجِبْ لَكُمْ

Say, "O My servants who have transgressed against themselves [by sinning], do not despair of the mercy of God. Indeed, God forgives all sins. Indeed, it is He who is the Forgiving, the Merciful."[57]

قُلْ يَا عِبَادِيَ الَّذِينَ أَسْرَفُوا عَلَى أَنْفُسِهِمْ لَا تَقْنَطُوا مِنْ رَحْمَةِ اللَّهِ إِنَّ اللَّهَ يَغْفِرُ الذُّنُوبَ جَمِيعًا إِنَّهُ هُوَ الْغَفُورُ الرَّحِيمُ

---

[56] Surah al-Ghafir 40:60.
[57] Surah as-Zumar 39:53.

Feel Allah's **Hayba!** – which means to have a sense of fear and awe paired with a deep reverence and veneration that one feels when standing in His hands. An example of a small element of Hayba is what is felt towards a parent or one in authority. Hayba is the highest level of fear. Recall the duas the Prophet ﷺ taught us which arouses in us this Hayba: *"There is no salvation from You except through You."* And *"I seek refuge in You, from You."* There are angels who have been in prostration and bowing since the day they were created and will remain so until the Day of Judgment, saying - *"Exalted are You, we have not worshiped You as You deserve to be worshiped.."*

With attributes such as "The Mighty", "The Compeller", "The [justifiably] Proud", "The Avenger"- the more you know about Allah [and the more you know about yourself in comparison to Him], the more Hayba you will feel towards Him. Everything is under His supremacy and His total control.

Who are we to defy His commands?! "What is the matter with you that you are not conscious of Allah's majesty.."[58] Allah Almighty addresses us all, "O mankind, it is you who are in need of Allah… If He wills, He can do away with you and bring forth a new creation."[59]

The Prophet was describing the Hayba angel Jibreel felt before His Lord on the night of Israa and Miraaj - He said, *"Jibreel was like a worn-out camel's cloth from the fear of Allah!"* Enter Salah with Great **Love** for Allah - For his beauty, for his kindness in dealing with you and for His favours and blessings upon you.

Feel a **shyness and a shame -** We commit much wrong but He continues to be so patient with us and he continues to cover and protect us despite all our transgressions. Allah says, *"Certainly will the believers have succeeded - They who during their prayer are humbly submissive."*[60]

The above secrets will help you attain that *"Khushu"*- that feeling of genuine humbleness and submissiveness that must be reached in Salah for you to benefit and succeed in this world and the next and for you to magnify the rewards of your prayer. Do you notice how the flood of thoughts and distrac-

---

[58] Surah Nuh 71:13.
[59] Surah Fatir 15-16.
[60] Surah al-Mu'minoon 23:1-2.

tions only comes once you start Salah [it's not present before]? It is this very Khushu' that Satan always tries to steal away from you in Salah. A thief would not bother stealing from a king's palace because it is well guarded, nor from a poor man's house because it is empty.

The house he always aims for is the rich man's house because it has the wealth, but without the guards. This is what you are. You are the rich man- You have the Khushu' [the wealth], but you don't have the guards that those who have reached Khushu's highest levels have [those of the palace]. And so Satan will keep trying to distract you to steal away from your prayer's worth. But as you start applying what you've learned from this series and as you begin to feel that happiness and peace that Salah was prescribed for, you will easily begin to overcome these distractions and the quality of your Salah will improve significantly.

Ask yourself, in which month do you feel you attain the most "khushu"? It is Ramadhan, isn't it? And during which time in Ramadhan, specifically? It is during the Taraweeh or night prayers, right? And in which segment of those prayers, in particular? It is during the dua at the end - where everyone raises their hands together and repeats a unified "Ameen" behind the Imam. That's when the eyes swell with tears and the sobs echo throughout the Masjid. Why at that moment do we feel the Khushu'? What is different in this segment of the prayer?

This is because at this moment, you suddenly *feel* that you are actually talking to Someone.. You realize that you are conversing with Allah directly! Therefore, to live these precious moments and achieve the needed Khushu' not just once a year, but in each and every Salah you perform everyday, feel with your total being that you are: **Talking** to Him - **Addressing** Him - **Conversing** with Him. Most people think Salah is a monologue and have forgotten that our Salah is really a *dialogue* from beginning to end. Live this dialogue - Feel the other side!